THE GREAT PLAGUE

Pamela Rushby

Illustrated by
Liz Alger

Cuisenaire
800-445-5985 www.etacuisenaire.com

The Great Plague

ISBN 978-0-7406-1201-5
ETA 620011

ETA/Cuisenaire • Vernon Hills, IL 60061-1862
800-445-5985 • www.etacuisenaire.com

Published by ETA/Cuisenaire® under license from
Pearson Australia (a division of Pearson Australia Group Pty Ltd)
All rights reserved.

Copyright © Pearson Australia 2010
(a division of Pearson Australia Group Pty Ltd)
Logo design © 2004 by ETA/Cuisenaire®

Text by Pamela Rushby
Edited by Philip Bryan
Designed by Cristina Neri Canary Graphic Design
Illustrated by Liz Alger

No part of this publication may be reproduced, stored in a
retrieval system, or transmitted, in any form or by any means,
electronic, mechanical, photocopying, recording, or otherwise,
without the prior written permission of the publisher.

Printed in China (SWTC/03)

11 12 13   10 9 8 7 6 5 4 3

Contents

Author's Note	1
CHAPTER 1 *The Plague Comes to Eyam*	3
CHAPTER 2 *Fleas and Patterns*	9
CHAPTER 3 *The Bad Times Begin*	13
CHAPTER 4 *Something Dark and Evil*	19
CHAPTER 5 *Eyam Is Cut Off*	26
CHAPTER 6 *The Worst Month*	35
CHAPTER 7 *The Boundary Stone*	42
CHAPTER 8 *Twenty-One Days Pass*	45
True and Terrible Tales	48
Eyam Today	58

Author's Note

This story is set in an English village called Eyam (pronounced *Eem*). The year is 1665. The plague—also known as the Black Death—has just reached Eyam from London.

This was a time of great change in England. After years of being ruled by strict Puritans, England had a king again, King Charles II. Things that had previously been banned—such as dancing and colourful clothes—were allowed once more.

Eyam is a real place, though some of the characters in this story are fictional. Robert and his family never lived in Eyam. But Pastor Thomas Stanley, Pastor William Mompesson and his wife Catherine, George Vicars, Jonathan Cooper and many others were real people. They lived in Eyam and died between 1665 and 1666.

Pamela Rushby

Chapter 1

The Plague Comes to Eyam

My name is Robert. My story starts on a summer afternoon in 1665. That was when the plague came to our little village. That was just eighteen months ago. It seems so long ago now, but when I count back, it really is just over a year and a half.

The plague came — and I saw it arrive.

I was on my way home after my lesson with Pastor Stanley. Pastor Stanley was teaching me to read and write. There weren't many boys in our village who could read and write.

But Pastor Stanley had told my mother and father that I was a bright boy and that I should learn to read and write. He'd said that he was willing to teach me.

"After all," he'd said. "I have time, now that I'm retired and the new pastor is here."

The Great Plague

My father didn't think much of reading and writing. "Robert will have our farm," he'd said to Pastor Stanley. "You don't need to read and write to run a farm!"

"But if Robert can read and write, he'll be able to keep the accounts," Pastor Stanley said.

My father listened to Pastor Stanley, but he still didn't say "yes".

Then my little sister, Anne, toddled across the kitchen. She put her hands on Pastor Stanley's knees and smiled up at him. Pastor Stanley looked at Anne, then he looked at my mother. "If Robert learns to read, he'll be able to read the Bible to you and Anne," he said. "He might even be able to teach little Anne to read."

That was that. My mother looked through the door into the parlour. Our big black Bible was kept carefully on a shelf in there. None of us could read it.

It didn't matter what my father thought about reading from then on. My mother had made up her mind.

"Robert is going to learn to read," she said. "And he might as well learn to write while he is at it."

So several times a week, after I'd done my work on the farm, I walked down the hill into Eyam, and had my lesson with Pastor Stanley.

Although, on a perfect summer day like this, I'd rather have been playing than learning how to read. I did not have much spare time. I could see my friend Jonathan Cooper over near the pond. I started running towards him.

Then I saw the carrier's horse and cart plod slowly down the main street. It wasn't every day that a letter or a parcel was delivered to Eyam. I stopped to watch.

The Great Plague

There was a passenger in the cart, too. I looked at the passenger out of the corner of my eye. I was curious, but it would be rude to stare. I couldn't see much of him anyway. The figure was sitting in the back of the cart, among the parcels and boxes. He was bent over as if he was weary—or as if he didn't want to be seen.

The figure was wrapped up in a black cloak, with the hood pulled down over his face. I thought that was odd, because it was such a warm afternoon. But I didn't think too much about it. After all, it was a sunny afternoon and I wanted to have some time with Jonathan. I ran towards him.

The cart stopped. The carrier took a parcel from the back of the cart and walked towards Jonathan's house.

"Look!" I said, as I reached Jonathan. "There's a parcel for your house!"

Jonathan looked towards his house. He wasn't very interested. "It'll be something for my stepfather's tailoring," he said.

Jonathan's mother had been widowed. She'd remarried not long ago. Her new husband was Alexander Hadfield. He was a tailor, and had come to live in Jonathan's house. His assistant, George Vicars, had come with him.

"George Vicars was talking about ordering some patterns for new clothes styles from London," said Jonathan. "That's probably what the carrier's delivering."

So the parcel was cloth or thread or tailor's patterns, I thought. It didn't seem very exciting.

When I looked back at the cart, the figure in the black hood was gone. "Who was that in the cart?" I asked. "Did you see him?"

"In the cart?" said Jonathan. "There's no-one in the cart."

"No, not now," I said. "But there was when it came in."

"I didn't see anyone," said Jonathan.

I glanced up and down the street, but the black-hooded figure was gone. There was no sign of him. Whoever it was must have moved quickly, I thought. Then I forgot about it. It wasn't important.

It was not until later that I saw the hooded figure again. And now, knowing what I could not possibly have known then, I can never get him out of my mind.

The figure haunts my dreams to this very day. I think I will feel haunted for the rest of my life.

CHAPTER 2

FLEAS AND PATTERNS

I played by the pond with Jonathan for the rest of the afternoon. When the shadows grew long, I knew it was time to go home. But I was thirsty. "Can I get a drink of water from your house before I walk home?" I asked.

"Of course," said Jonathan.

We walked back to Jonathan's house together. It was one of four houses standing together in a little group near the churchyard.

As we walked towards it, I saw the black figure again. He was at the open door of Jonathan's house.

He looked in, and then he went inside. Once again, I wondered who he was. Strangers weren't common in Eyam. But I'd see for myself in a moment.

The Great Plague

When we reached Jonathan's house, everything inside was bustle and confusion. Although it was still a warm day, the fire in the kitchen was blazing high. Damp pieces of cloth were draped over every piece of furniture and dangling from strings across the room. As we walked in, George Vicars and Jonathan's mother were spreading more pieces of cloth to dry.

"What's happened?" asked Jonathan.

"It's my patterns from London," said George Vicars. He sounded annoyed. "The parcel's been left in the rain. Everything's damp! I'm trying to dry the patterns before people come to look at the new styles."

"And look!" complained Mrs Hadfield. "There's even fleas in them! Fleas!"

I backed away. Fleas weren't all that unusual. But my mother would not be very

happy if I brought fleas into our clean house.

"I won't stay," I said. "I'd better get home."

It wasn't until I was running up the hill to our house that I thought about the black figure again. He hadn't been in Jonathan's kitchen. So where had he gone? Had he gone to talk with Jonathan's stepfather? Now I would never know who Jonathan's visitor had been. Oh, well—it was really none of my business anyway.

I didn't have a lesson with Pastor Stanley for a few days, so I didn't go back into Eyam. But my father went into the village to attend to some business.

The Great Plague

After my father walked home, he sat down to pull his boots off. "I heard some news in the village," he said. "About the tailor's assistant, George Vicars."

"Yes?" said my mother.

"He's dead," said my father. "He died yesterday, after a sudden sickness. The funeral was today."

"God rest his soul, poor man," said my mother.

And then they talked of other things. George Vicars wasn't from Eyam and he hadn't lived there long. His death wasn't as important to us as that of someone we knew well.

So George Vicars died, and was buried, and that was the end of him.

However, it was just the beginning for Eyam. It was only two weeks later that the bad times began.

The Bad Times Begin

One evening, I snatched some time away from my work. I went into the village to play with Jonathan and some other boys. I went into Eyam again the next evening for my lesson with Pastor Stanley. As I passed Jonathan's house, I saw that the door was shut and the windows were covered. That was unusual. In warm weather, house doors were open all day long. Had Jonathan's family left the village for the day?

It was bad news. Pastor Stanley looked upset when I arrived at his house. "You should know about your friend Jonathan," he said. "Jonathan could need some comfort from you, Robert."

"Why?" I asked anxiously. "What's happened?"

"It's his brother, Edward," said Pastor Stanley. "Edward died today."

The Great Plague

I stared at him. "Edward!" I said. "But Edward can't be dead! I saw him yesterday. There was nothing wrong with him!"

"It was very sudden," said Pastor Stanley. "He was ill this morning, and he died just an hour ago."

I still couldn't believe it. I shook my head.

"We'll have no lesson today," said Pastor Stanley kindly. "Go and see Jonathan." He paused.

"But, Robert," he said. "Don't go into the house. Don't go to see Edward's body, even if they ask you to. Stay outside."

The Bad Times Begin

He said this softly, watching me as he spoke. I knew that he meant what he said, and that he had good reason for saying it, but he wasn't going to say what that reason was.

"I won't go in," I said.

I went to the house and saw Jonathan, but I don't know if I was much comfort to him. He looked stunned, as if he couldn't believe what had happened either. I heard his mother crying inside.

I didn't stay long. I went home and told my parents about it. My mother got up at once. "I must go and see his poor mother," she said.

I hesitated. If my mother was going to the village, she should know what Pastor Stanley had told me. "Pastor Stanley told me that I was not to go into that house," I said.

My parents stared at each other. "What reason did he give?" asked my father.

"None," I said. "But he meant what he said."

"He thinks the illness is catching," my mother said. She looked anxiously at Anne and me. "I'll be very careful."

The Great Plague

So my mother went to see Edward's mother and tried to give her some comfort.

The next week, my mother went to the village, on the same sad errand, again and again. Because in the next week, four more people died: Peter Hawksworth, Thomas Thorpe and his daughter Mary, then Sarah Syddall.

We heard, too, that Mary Thorpe and Elizabeth Thorpe were both very sick. Six people, who had seemed healthy, had died in three weeks. And others were sick.

All of the dead and sick people had lived very close to each other, in the little cluster of four cottages near the churchyard.

Everyone was afraid. What could have caused so many deaths? That was when the word *plague* was first whispered.

"Plague!" said my mother. Her face went white.

"It's best not to go into the village again for a while," said my father.

"No," said my mother. "No, I won't. But the plague! Why should the plague have come here?"

The Bad Times Begin

We had known that there was plague in London. But London was 150 miles away. We had thought we were safe. Why had the plague come here?

It was the question everyone was asking. What could we have done wrong that such a sickness should come to us?

Some people, who followed the old Puritan religion, said that the wrath of God had come to strike us down. They said God was angry with us because we'd started to follow the ways of the new Pastor, William Mompesson.

Others thought back to a prank some boys had played a few months ago. The boys had let a cow and her calf into the church, and chased them around inside it.

The poor frightened animals had dirtied the floor before someone had led them out. Some people said the village was being punished for allowing such a thing to take place in the church.

Others said they'd heard the Gabriel hounds howling in the sky one night. The Gabriel hounds were supposed to be the souls of children who'd died unbaptised. To hear their cry meant doom. And one old woman said she'd seen white crickets in front of her fireplace. Everyone knew, she said, that white crickets meant bad luck.

"Nonsense!" said Pastor Stanley. "It's a sickness. No-one knows why it comes. Or," he added softly, "where it'll go next."

But I found that I knew where it was going to go next.

Something Dark and Evil

I had another lesson with Pastor Stanley that evening. When I was coming home, I passed the Syddalls' house. Sarah Syddall had died in the house that day.

That's when I saw the black figure.

He came out of the Syddalls' house and walked slowly into the street. His hooded head moved from side to side. It was as if the figure was looking for the next place he wanted to go.

He walked up to the door of the Thorpes' house. He looked around again. This time his head turned towards me. I could see him clearly. And there was nothing inside the hood. Nothing! No face, no head, just a terrible black emptiness.

I had never been so afraid in my life. What was *it*? There seemed to be nothing inside that cloak and hood, but I knew that something dark and evil was watching me.

I couldn't move. The black figure looked at me for a moment, then it turned away. It raised its arm, pushed open the Thorpes' door and went in.

In seconds, I heard a cry from the Thorpes' house. "She's gone!" a voice wailed. "Mary's gone!"

I knew then what I'd just seen. I'd seen the Black Death itself. The black figure was the plague, and it was in our village. It had been here for weeks. I'd seen it arrive. I'd seen it go to Jonathan's house before George Vicars and Edward had died. I'd seen it come from the Syddalls' house, where Sarah had died. Now it was at the Thorpes' house. And I was sure that

Mary Thorpe, too, had just died.

I dropped to the ground on my knees. I was shaking.

Pastor Stanley came out of the churchyard. "Robert!" he cried. "Robert! What is it? Are you sick?" He took my arm and helped me up, looking anxiously into my face.

I told him what I'd seen. "It's the Black Death itself!" I said. "It's here! We have to tell everyone!"

Pastor Stanley was very stern with me. "The plague is a sickness, not a black figure," he said. "People are already frightened enough, without a boy telling stories about seeing the Black Death.

"Go home, Robert. And don't frighten anyone by telling such wicked stories."

"I'm sorry," I said, even though I was quite sure about what I'd seen. "I won't frighten anyone."

I went home. I didn't tell anyone else about the black figure, not even my parents. But it didn't need stories from me to frighten people.

People began to leave the village. Some families were lucky enough to have another house or farm that they could go to. They packed up their belongings and left.

But other people had nowhere to go. Some of them decided to leave anyway, and live in barns or huts on the hills. Most people had no choice in the matter and stayed in the village.

Our farm was on a hill high above the village. My parents felt that we were at least as safe as those people who were living in the fields. If we kept away from the village as much as we could, perhaps we'd be all right.

"What about Robert's lessons?" said my mother.

My father was a man who thought that once you'd started something, you should keep at it. "If he goes straight to and from Pastor Stanley's, he'll be all right," he said.

My mother wasn't so sure. "What if it gets worse?" she asked. "He can't keep going to the village if the sickness gets worse."

And it did get worse.

In October, twenty-three more people died. Not everyone took the sickness in the same way. Some died in an hour; others lingered for three or four days.

This is what happened to them.

At the first moment of catching the plague, some people saw strange lights, or believed they could hear sweet voices singing. A few could smell a sweet, lingering scent in the air.

But others heard or saw or smelt nothing. They simply felt sick and feverish, and didn't want their food.

Some, like Edward, died very quickly.

The Great Plague

Those who didn't die quickly became more ill over the next few days. Swellings appeared in their groin, neck, elbows or armpits. They were tight, hard, red swellings that grew to the size of an apple, and were painful to the touch.

Sometimes, the swellings would burst open and pus would leak out. If this happened, the victims might recover. If it didn't, the victims' noses began to bleed, and angry red marks appeared on their bodies, like blood trapped under the skin. Their fever grew higher and higher until—after three or four days—they died.

Twenty-three people died in this way in October. One of them was my friend Jonathan. And still people died.

Not as many people died in the cold months. We'd expected this, because the plague was a sickness of the warmer seasons. But, by April, seventy-three people from Eyam had died.

I saw the black figure again and again as I walked through the village. Nobody else ever mentioned it. I realised they couldn't see it, and I knew better than to tell anyone about it now.

I watched the figure as it moved from one house to another. I kept as far away from it as I could. Sometimes, I saw it watching me, and I shivered. Did it know that only I, in the whole village, could see it? Or was it waiting for the right moment—to come for me?

Eyam Is Cut Off

May came. The weather grew warmer. Summer was coming. The village held its breath and waited to see whether the sickness would strike again.

In May, although the days were warmer, only two people died. We couldn't believe it. Could it be over? We knew we had to wait for twenty-one days to pass, without any new case of the plague, before we could consider that the sickness was over. We waited and we hoped in vain.

In June, nineteen people died. The plague had returned—and it was worse than ever.

It was at this time that Pastor Mompesson and Pastor Stanley called a village meeting. They had a plan.

I haven't said much about Pastor Mompesson. My family followed the old religion.

Eyam Is Cut Off

Pastor Mompesson's ways were very strange to us. Pastor Mompesson was young, only twenty-eight, and much freer in his ways, and in the style and colour of his clothing, than Pastor Stanley. In the village, some families preferred Pastor Stanley's old religion; others preferred the new style of Pastor Mompesson.

The two pastors were not friends, but they were both good, intelligent men. They realised that they would have to act together to get the whole village to agree to their plan. So, when a meeting of the whole village was called, it was the old pastor and the new pastor acting together.

The Great Plague

What the pastors had to suggest astounded and frightened us all. They stood before us in the church and waited until everyone had come in. Then they spoke.

With our consent, they said, they had a plan that might prevent the plague from spreading further. They had three suggestions to put to us.

First, they said, there should be no more proper funerals, and no more burials in the churchyard. This was because too many people were dying. There was no more room in the churchyard, and the pastors needed their time to help the living.

Instead, families should bury their dead in their own gardens or fields, digging the graves themselves.

Second, the church would be closed and services held in the open air. If, as most people thought, the plague was spread by vapours, or germs, in the air, then it made sense that we shouldn't stand close to each other in the church.

The pastors suggested using a place called Cucklett Delph, a large dell with high, grassy slopes on three sides and a stream flowing out of it on the other. There was a tall rock, Pastor Mompesson said, that could be used as a pulpit.

The pastors paused. Then they straightened their shoulders and went on. Third, they said, everyone who lived in the village was asked to promise to stay within the village. They were not to go to other towns, or even pass the parish boundaries. If we agreed to do that, the pastors said, they hoped that the plague would be prevented from spreading to other towns.

There was complete silence in the church. Then there was an uproar. Everyone started asking questions. Why should we do this? Why should we cut ourselves off? We'd all die! The pastors had an answer for that. The plague was already within our village, they said. It was already too late for us. But, for others, in the nearby towns, it wasn't too late. Could we bear to have it on our consciences if we took the plague to other people?

The Great Plague

There was silence for a while. Many people had family and friends in nearby towns.

Then more questions. Food, people demanded. How would we get food?

The pastors had thought of that, too. The Earl of Devonshire, who lived nearby, had agreed that he would supply bread and meat and medical supplies to Eyam. The food would be left at places at the parish boundaries each day.

If we wanted anything special, the pastors said, the Earl's servants would get it for us if we left money early in the morning at the boundaries. The money should be put in a jar of vinegar, to keep the plague from spreading. The goods could be collected at midday.

There was silence while people thought about this. Then there were more questions, more arguments and more questions.

The pastors said that everyone had to agree if the plan was to work.

By late afternoon, everyone had agreed. Many of the men were scowling. Many of

the women were crying. But all agreed there was little else that could be done.

Silently, everyone left the church and went to their homes. The black figure was standing outside the churchyard wall. I wondered if it had had to stand outside while we made our decision, because it couldn't enter a holy place.

The Great Plague

"*Maybe this will stop you!*" I thought, as I walked as far around it as I could. "*Surely what the whole village is about to do will stop you!*"

But, as I walked by, although I could hear nothing, I was sure that the black figure, deep inside its hood, was laughing.

Chapter 6

The Worst Month

The black figure had had good reason to laugh.

We did everything the two pastors had suggested. And they'd been right in one way. The plague didn't spread to nearby towns. But it became even worse in our village.

That summer was a hot, sticky, breathless one. More and more people became sick every day.

In July, fifty-six people died.

August was the worst month. In August, seventy-eight people died in Eyam.

Then, in September, the most terrible thing of all happened.

I came home from my lesson one evening, running up the hill to our farm. The days were getting shorter, and there was a feeling of autumn in the air.

The Great Plague

When the cold weather came, we knew that the plague was likely to lessen, just as it had last winter. We were all waiting anxiously for winter.

I pushed open the kitchen door and looked around for my little sister, Anne.

Anne was sitting on the floor in front of the fire. And sitting on a low stool beside her, with its hood bent towards her, was the black figure.

For a moment, I couldn't move. Then I shouted, "No! No!"

Anne looked up. My mother swung around, startled. My father stared at me.

"No!" I shouted again. I snatched Anne up from the floor and threw her into my mother's arms.

I flung myself at the black figure. I wanted to fight it, to fling it out of our house, to destroy it. But my hands touched nothing. There was nothing there to take hold of, even though I could see the figure perfectly clearly by our fire.

I fell back. What could I do? I couldn't fight something I couldn't feel!

The Great Plague

Then the black figure raised its head and looked at me. I saw the terrible emptiness within its hood again. I heard its words, not with my ears, but inside my head.

"Not you," it said. "Not you."

"No!" I shouted again. My mother and father were staring at me, horrified. Anne was crying. I knew they couldn't see the black figure. All they could see was me, their Robert, acting as if I was mad. Inside my head, I heard the black figure laugh and laugh.

I couldn't bear it. I ran to the door, pushing my father aside, and bolted out. I ran and ran. I knew what was going to happen in my home. There was nothing I could do about it. But I didn't want to see it.

I heard my parents calling after me. I realised they thought that *I* was sick. They searched for me, but I ran and ran up into the hills.

I don't know how far I ran. I don't know how many days I was away. I remember drinking water from streams, but I don't know what I ate or how I got it. Perhaps some of the people who were living in the barns and huts on the hills gave me food.

Days and nights went by. When I thought it must have been a week, I knew enough time had passed. I must go home.

I stumbled down the hill towards our house. There was no smoke coming from the chimney. The door was swinging open, and hens were walking in and out of the kitchen. Inside, the fire was out and the ashes were cold. Slowly, I went towards the stairs. I already knew what I'd find upstairs.

The Great Plague

I buried Anne, my mother and my father in the garden. Then I found a large, flat stone and scratched their initials and the date on it. I set the stone at the head of the grave.

And that was all I could do for them. When I'd finished, I sat beside the grave and stared at it. I sat there all night.

In the morning, Pastor Stanley came. He put his hand out and helped me to my feet. Then, without a word, he put his arm around my shoulders and took me home with him.

"I ran away," I said. "I ran away and left them."

"You couldn't have done anything, Robert," he said softly.

"I could have stayed," I said.

He looked into my face. "If you want to, if you think it will help, you can do something for others."

So I did. I helped Pastor Stanley for the rest of September and all of October. I washed faces, gave drinks of water and carried basins. But I did this for others, not for my own family.

The Boundary Stone

Altogether, twenty-four people died in September.

The plague ended in October 1666.

All that month, fewer and fewer people had become sick. Many of those who became sick recovered. Only fourteen people died in October.

And then, no more died. It was over.

On the first day of November, I saw the black figure for the last time. It was a day of low clouds and grey, misty rain.

It was walking down the middle of the street, on the way out of the village. I watched it dully. I wondered who would be next, which door it would stop at.

But it didn't stop. It walked and walked. I realised that it was reaching the outskirts of the village.

The Boundary Stone

There were no more houses in front of it, but it still kept walking. I followed slowly behind it. It walked and walked, past the boundary stone, and up the hill.

I stopped beside the boundary stone. I knew I mustn't go past it. The black figure reached the top of the hill. Then it paused. It turned to look down towards Eyam. I saw the terrible black emptiness inside its hood. Then it turned away, walked over the hill—and was gone.

I stared after it for a long time. It didn't come back. At last, I turned around and went back into the village.

I walked slowly down the street, looking around. It was as if I hadn't seen my village for a long, long time. I looked at it as if I'd just come back from a journey. It seemed deserted.

The Great Plague

There was no smoke coming from most of the chimneys. Grass grew between the cobbles of the street, where no feet had walked to wear it away. A cow wandered down the middle of the street, and no-one chased it or came to claim it and put it back in its field. Doors on many of the houses swung open onto empty, echoing rooms.

I hadn't cried since I'd buried my family. But now I started to cry again.

Only one person moved in the whole village. Pastor Stanley was walking towards me. When he had almost reached me, I stumbled towards him.

"Robert!" he said. "What is it? What's happened?"

I fell into his arms. "It's gone," I said. "The plague's over! It's gone!"

Chapter 8

Twenty-One Days Pass

It took time for people to believe that the plague had really gone. Twenty-one days passed without anyone dying. Twenty-one days without a death was the number of days needed before Eyam could be declared plague-free. Even then, people were reluctant to believe that it was over. But more days passed and all was well.

It was almost winter. We knew that the warm months were the plague months. Perhaps we were safe for now. But would the plague return next summer?

Pastor Mompesson told everyone that we should burn anything that might have the seeds of the plague still in it: clothing, sheets and blankets. Perhaps, that way, we could destroy any remaining danger. He set an example by burning almost everything he owned.

People followed Pastor Mompesson's lead. Fires burned in the street day and night, and smoke hung low. We coughed in the smoke as we fed the fires, and our eyes turned red and sore. But perhaps it wasn't just the smoke that made our eyes red. We had all lost so much.

It's almost Christmas now, but it won't be a merry one. Some of the people who left the village have returned. Once, three hundred people lived in Eyam. Today there are only forty-one people left. We're all trying to make up our minds what to do.

I'm still living with Pastor Stanley. He says I'm welcome to stay as long as I like. But there's the farm on the hill. It's my farm now.

Twenty-One Days Pass

I don't know if I can bear to live on the farm alone. I haven't been back since I buried my family. But it's still my place, my home. My father wanted me to have it. One day soon, I'll go up there and see what's happened to the house since it's been empty. And see if I can live there and make a new life for myself.

I still don't know why I was the only one, in the whole village, who could see the Black Death. I wish I hadn't been. Because I know I will see it in my dreams for the rest of my life.

The End

True and Terrible Tales

Terrible things happened in Eyam in those years. Here are some of the true and terrible tales.

The Tale of Marshall Howe

MARSHALL HOWE

Marshall Howe was a miner from the village. He was a big, strong, loud man. Marshall was one of the first people to catch the plague, but his attack was only light and he recovered. He knew it was very unlikely he'd catch the plague again.

When the plague was at its worst, it sometimes happened that there was no-one left in a family to dig the grave. The last person left might be too old, or too young or too sick to do it. That was when Marshall Howe stepped in.

"I'll dig the grave," said Marshall. "I'll take care of the burial, too." And so he did. But it was the way that Marshall took care of the burial that offended and upset people.

If a person was very sick, Marshall would begin digging the grave at once. But he often dug it in the garden, right outside the window of the dying person, who would hear him at work.

When it was time for the burial, Marshall would roughly drag the body to the grave, without dignity or respect. When he'd finished, Marshall would come back to the house and take anything he fancied. "It's my payment," he'd say.

No-one liked having Marshall bury members of their family, but some people had no choice.

At the end of August, Marshall Howe entered one infected house too many. He didn't become sick himself, but he took the seeds of the plague home with him. Within days, his wife Joan and son William were dead.

Marshall Howe never dug another grave.

The Tale of the Talbots and the Hancocks

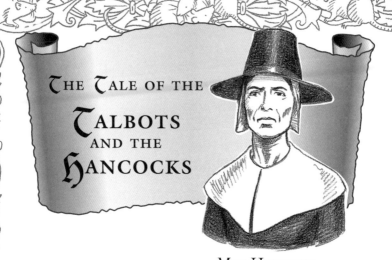

Mrs Hancock

The Talbots and the Hancocks were two families who lived away from the village. Their farms were up in the hills, side by side. They probably thought they would be safe from the plague.

But, in July, the plague came to the Talbot family. There were eleven members of the Talbot family. Ten of them died, one after the other, in just over three weeks. Only the old grandmother was left.

When the last Talbot child died, the grandmother was unable to bury him. Robert Hancock came from the next farm to bury the boy. Finally, in August, the old grandmother died herself. By then the Hancocks had caught the plague.

Mrs Hancock was the only member of the family who was healthy. As her family lay sick, Mrs Hancock dug their graves and buried them, one by one.

People walking to the boundary stone below the hill to collect food, or to leave requests and money, could look up and see Mrs Hancock. Day after day, she dug one grave after another and dragged her family out to them. She buried her husband and her six children in just one week.

The Tale of the Runaway

THE RUNAWAY

Only one person tried to run away from Eyam during the time that everyone agreed not to leave the village.

She was a woman from a part of the village called Orchard Bank. She made up her mind to escape.

She left the village without anyone seeing her and made her way to the next village, Tideswell. It was market day in Tideswell. She hoped that there would be so many people in the town that she wouldn't be noticed.

The people of Tideswell had put a guard on the road outside the town. The guard asked her where she was from. Instead of saying "Eyam", she said "Orchard Bank". The guard let her through.

She thought she was safe—but she was recognised by some people in the marketplace.

"A woman from Eyam!" they cried. They chased her through the town and threw vegetables and stones at her. Finally, they chased her past the guard and back onto the road to Eyam.

She returned to her house, bruised and frightened. She never tried to leave Eyam again.

THE CARTER

One man entered Eyam by mistake.

He was a carter with a load of timber. Somehow no-one saw him or warned him away, and he came into the village with his load.

It was a rainy day and he was wet, but he started to unload his cart. People watched from their windows, thinking they had better stay away from him. He was soaked through by the time he'd finished unloading. He went back home to his village, Bubnell.

The next day he was feverish and sneezing. The people of Bubnell were horrified, and told him to stay in his house. They went to the Earl of Devonshire, who sent his own doctor to find out if the carter had brought the plague from Eyam.

TRUE AND TERRIBLE TALES

The doctor didn't want to get close to the carter. He told the carter to come out of his house and to cross the bridge to the other side of the river. The doctor walked along the river bank until he was opposite the carter. The doctor stayed on his side of the river and called across it, asking the carter questions about his symptoms.

Finally, the doctor decided that the carter had only caught a feverish cold. All was well. The plague had not come to their village.

The Tale of Catherine Mompesson

CATHERINE MOMPESSON

Catherine Mompesson was the pretty young wife of Pastor Mompesson. She had sent her two young children away to live with relatives soon after the plague began. She had asked Pastor Mompesson if they could all leave, but he'd refused. "I must stay," he said. So Catherine stayed with him.

Catherine worked day and night caring for the sick people. She visited them, took them food and drink, and made them comfortable. She went into many plague houses, but she didn't catch the plague herself.

Until August. One evening, Catherine and Pastor Mompesson were walking home after a long day of visiting the sick. Catherine took a deep breath. "How sweet the air smells tonight!" she said.

The air probably did smell sweet after a day spent in plague houses, but Pastor Mompesson was suddenly afraid. One symptom of the plague was that people sometimes thought they could smell a sweet fragrance in the air.

Catherine had caught the plague. She died a few days later.

Because Catherine had worked so hard for the sick, special permission was given to bury her body in the churchyard.

Eyam Today

The village of Eyam is in Derbyshire, England. It is 240 kilometres from London. About 1000 people live there today.

If you visit Eyam, you can see the old houses where some of the victims of the plague lived. They are known as the "Plague Cottages". There are plaques on some of the cottages that record the names of some of the first people to die.

There is a museum in the village that tells the story of the plague years.

You can still see the boundary stones outside Eyam. These are the stones where food was left for the villagers, and where they left their money, soaking in vinegar.

Eyam Today

The last Sunday in August is known as Plague Sunday in Eyam. A special church service is held on that day every year. The service commemorates the bravery of the people of Eyam during the plague. A procession of local people, led by a band, marches to Cucklett Delph, where open-air church services were held during the plague. A church service is held there in memory of the people who died.

Eyam Today

On Plague Sunday, red roses can always be found on Catherine Mompesson's tomb. She was one of the very few plague victims to be buried in the churchyard. Until her death, she had worked tirelessly for the sick. Special permission was given for her burial in the churchyard. Every year on Plague Sunday, the wife of the present church minister places red roses on Catherine Mompesson's tomb.